CONFIDENCE, LIPSTICK AND CRIMINAL JUSTICE

A GUIDE FOR COLLEGE WOMEN STARTING IN CRIMINAL JUSTICE

DeNaye' Dotson

Copyright © 2020 DeNaye' Dotson

All rights reserved. No part of this publication may be reproduced, stored in a retrieval system, or transmitted, in any form or by any means, electronic, mechanical, photocopying, recording, or otherwise, without the prior written permission of the publisher.

Printed in the United States of America.

For more information and inquiries, address DeNaye' Dotson at PO Box 153 Akron Ohio 44309

ISBN 9781735517803

Write To Bless LLC Publishing

DEDICATION

In loving memory of **Patricia M. Alexander**, my loving Aunt: Who loved her family and serving the community. Who always smiled with her perfectly applied lipstick every day. The confidence she got when she wore it and the sense of direction. That meant she was getting ready for business. I remember, my Aunt would put on the lipstick every time we got in the car. Using the rearview mirror to apply her lipstick, to me that symbolized how she used the rearview mirror not to look back but to prepare for moving forward.

She would tell everyone to go for their goals and take action. I am still going, with my lipstick on!

ACKNOWLEDGMENTS

My First of many books! I must thank: -God- Thank you for using me to serve the people. Thank you for walking with me through this life journey and the protection, teaching, favor, positioning, and opening doors that only you could provide. **-Mom and Dad-** Thank you for your prayers and cheering for me. Love you. **-Aunt Pat-** I will always remember you putting on your lipstick and the many joyous memories. I miss you so much!**-Alesha-** Thank you cousin for your input and support during this book journey love you. **-Taurea Avant-** Thank you Coach for your instruction, certifying me and push to finish this book! Special thanks to **Brittany** of Bold Editing LLC (IG:_Boldediting).

TABLE OF CONTENTS

DEDICATION i
ACKNOWLEDGMENTS ii
INTRODUCTION 7
CHAPTER 1 MINDSET, LIPSTICK AND CONFIDENCE 9
    MINDSET AND LIPSTICK 9
    ELIMINATE NEGATIVE WORDS 10
    EMBRACE THE POSITIVE 12
    MENTAL TOUGHNESS 13
    CONFIDENCE 14
CHAPTER 2 YOUR OOTD (OUTFIT OF THE DAY) 18
    WHAT ARE YOU WEARING? 18
    CLOTHING AND ACCESSORIES 19
    HAIR AND MAKEUP 23
CHAPTER 3 CRIMINAL JUSTICE 25
    WORK-LIFE BALANCE 25
    WOMEN IN THE LAW 25
    WORKING IN CRIMINAL JUSTICE FIELD SYNOPSIS 28
    THE THREE COMPONENTS 31
    WHAT AREA OF CRIMINAL JUSTICE INTEREST YOU? 32
    THE CAMPAIGN TRAIL 33
    CRIMINAL JUSTICE FINAL THOUGHT 34
    HISTORY POINTS OF THE CRIMINAL JUSTICE SYSTEM 35
CHAPTER 4 APPLY 46
    ROLES AND RESPONSIBILITIES 46
    APPLY FOR THE POSITION 47

- INTERNSHIP VS FIELD EXPERIENCE 48
- CHAPTER 5 EVALUATION 49
  - EVALUATIONS 49
  - EVALUATION FACTORS 50
- CHAPTER 6 STAY ALERT 52
  - LISTEN TO YOUR GUT.. 52
  - BE AWARE OF YOUR SURROUNDINGS 53
  - STAY CALM, THINK SMART, SMALL TALK 56
  - KEEP YOUR INFORMATION PRIVATE 57
- CHAPTER 7 GETTING HELP 58
  - PROTECTION ORDER 58
  - POLICE REPORT 59
- FINAL NOTE 60
- THE AUTHOR'S CRIMINAL JUSTICE EXPERIENCE 62
- APPENDIX 65
- REFERENCES 76

INTRODUCTION

Confidence is a key foundation of what we think about ourselves. That level of self-worth will shine forth in everything we do, even if there are challenges to succeed. It is the aura when we walk in the room and it manifests in our speech. Overall, confidence is needed on the journey of any career field.

Why lipstick? A lady has to look good, right? When wearing a uniform, a suit, heels or sandals, appearance matters. Period. However, being a woman does not negate the powers or abilities to perform, and it eliminates any myths concerning this double standard. Makeup is used to enhance or cover up. When it comes to mindset we must decorate your thoughts like applying makeup. Remove the negative and replace it with a positive way of thinking, wink with mental toughness and smile with confidence. What we think will manifest in our face and body language speaks to the world.

And lastly, Criminal justice, which is also known as the career field that never sleeps. This field genuinely shows great levels of servanthood, protection, and respect. While working in the criminal justice field, you learn a lot about the behaviors of people, and yet, you often reflect on your self-morals.

These three topics: confidence, lipstick, and criminal justice, make up a woman. A woman must be confident when facing challenges in their daily lives. She wears lipstick to show the feminine side of being a woman who appreciates beauty and is also beautiful. Then, there is the criminal justice field to help serve, respect, and protect our family neighbors and the entire community.

"Justice consists in righteousness reasonableness and fairness. The sense of justice influences and controls human behavior." –Dr. T.P. Chia

My experience, and tips on these topics, and things I wish I would have known, are addressed within the pages of this book. I hope this book will shed some light and provide a better perspective for women desiring to work in this field.

CHAPTER 1
MINDSET, LIPSTICK AND CONFIDENCE

"You need to learn how to select your thoughts just the same way you select your clothes every day. This is a power you can cultivate. If you want to control things in your life so bad, work on the mind. That's the only thing you should be trying to control."

— *The Movie: Eat, Pray, Love*

MINDSET AND LIPSTICK

In ancient times, Egyptians used the dust of crushed gemstones to add color to enhance their face. In other terms, the use of what we now call "makeup." In a comparison of mindset and makeup think of it as decorating our thoughts in a way of positivity, pleasantness, and patience. What we think is what we will be and project to the world. Our mindset is everything!

When applying makeup, using different techniques, and colors the same method would be used to select the right positive thoughts for the best outcomes. Having a positive mindset will help you be more receptive to learning and receive knowledge, which results in a boost of confidence.

ELIMINATE NEGATIVE WORDS

"We hear ourselves say things, and then our subconscious takes in those messages, internalizing them. It's a vicious cycle, or a good one, depending on what you say."

— *Madame Noire*

Eliminate negative words as soon as they pop into your mind. We do not realize the unhealthy mental patterns and the self-defeating words we speak. For example, words such as I can't, but I'll fail, I won't make the mark. These are just a few keywords that close our minds to solutions, and in other words, put limitations on ourselves. These are a few of the many negative phrases of assumptions that repeat in our minds.

So, replace "I can't" and "but" with "How could I (fill in the blank". This will help boost your confidence.

By being more cautious, we will see a subconscious effort to do more things than make excuses.

Madame Noire further mentioned the reasons to remove the negative phrase sayings and why:

- **People are the worst-** Saying this regularly will put a negative lens on the way you interpret all actions of others.

- **This would happen to me-** Many things happen to a lot of people every day. This phrase carries the idea that you are cursed in some way or things are not supposed to work out for you. That mentality will not get you far.

- **I am not good at <u>insert skill</u>-** When you tell yourself that you are not good at anything, you remove the most important thing you need to be good at any of those: confidence.

- **That's just the way things are-** If you are telling yourself that, then you will never make any attempts to change things. Things will stay just as they are, but not because they were unchangeable, but rather because you did nothing about it.

- **That person doesn't like me-** There may be a lot of people you encounter every day who you believe do not like you.

    Maybe it is because they did not talk to you, smile, or say much. So now you have decided that after one interaction they do not like you and, for all you know, they are shy, depressed, or stressed out.

- **What's even the point? -** This phrase and attitude is a slippery slope. By asking this question, when it comes to anything, and life does not give you an immediate answer as to what the point is, the reverse is to go for the things, and the point will manifest itself.

- **I am going to mess this up-** When you get accepted for a job, or a special position in your life and you tell yourself, you are going to mess this up. This is a form of self-fulfilling prophesy. Meaning, you have concluded that you will mess it up and this will stop you from putting effort in believing it would be all for nothing, in which messes things up.

EMBRACE THE POSITIVE

To create healthy patterns in our minds we must stop, breathe, and set our minds to things that give us peace and joy. The key to this is disciplining our minds. Train your mind to think positively instead of being entangled with a negative thought. A technique to challenge the negative and embracing the positive is by writing all the negative statements that come to mind on one side of the paper and write the positive (an affirmation) on the other side. Then, finally, recite the affirmations throughout the day. This is a guaranteeing way to a positive mindset.

MENTAL TOUGHNESS

"The strength of your mind determines the quality of your life." -Unknown

Mental toughness is said to be more valuable than intelligence and skill. Working in the criminal justice field, your mental health and wellness are especially important. The stress and the stress response, concentration, stress management, and how to cope with high stressful traumatic situations are important and can weigh heavily on the mental state of an individual in this field. Case studies states:

"Mental toughness describes a set of attributes relating to how individuals deal with challenges, stressors, and pressures...[also] was found to be significantly related to perceived stress, with control of emotion, control of life, and

confidence in abilities being particularly important. There was no consistent relationship of age, rank, or length of service with mental toughness and perceived stress."

– Emerald Insight.

Mental toughness is used to resist weakness, overcome obstacles. Some key factors are determination, consistency, and perseverance to keep striving through while moving forward. To make your mind strong, you must take action. It does not suddenly happen for you with some sort of prayer, working out, or at a certain timeframe. It must be proven. Mental toughness is like a muscle. It needs to be worked to grow and developed by individual choices daily. If you have not stretched yourself to put yourself out there, or by trying things in many small ways, you will crumple when faced with difficult challenges. So, a way to be mentally fit is to develop systems that help you keep focused on the things that are important while you are moving forward.

CONFIDENCE

What is confidence anyway? Confidence is believing in yourself and reinforcing it with a skill.

"Confidence is an essential quality to have not only to better your career, but also to take care of yourself as a whole person."

– The Importance of Confidence In The Workplace– by Kariann Gills

There may be a time of conflict in your life journey with a coworker or a customer, or another stressful moment that creates anxiety and insecurity within. This is when you will need to rely on confidence. It will help you stay grounded and less frustrated, so you can solve the issue and get through the challenge strong and successful. A positive attitude is everything. The mind is a powerful thing!

Tips to confidence at work:

1. **Boost your knowledge-** Read more, dive deeper into how and why the process is the way it is, or how it came to be.
2. **Correct mistakes along the way.**
3. **Build your strengths-** Focus on your strengths, accept what you are good at, and strengthen those great qualities of yourself. When you complete a task improve more on it next time

4. **Eliminate negative words and negative self-talk-** Remove *"I can't, I can't do this, but it's not going to work."* This will lower your confidence and you will be limiting your chances of succeeding.
5. **Stop beating yourself up with negative self-talk on the mistakes you made-** Remove *"I can't, I can't do this, but it's not going to work."* This will lower your confidence and you will be limiting your chances of succeeding.
6. **Asking questions-** It is a key to our lives. When we do not know something, we should not be timid. Speak up and ask for help. If we do not fully understand something and we continue in fear of asking for help, then we are not boosting our confidence.
7. **Fake it until you make it-** Take a deep breath, think positive, and just do it! Knowing you will succeed in the task at hand. By instantly acting confidently, you will realize how capable and how dedicated a person you are.
8. **Focus on your successes-** Think about all great projects (tasks), things you have accomplished, and how your coworkers cheered for your idea and

accomplishment, or remember how you pressed through the challenges to successfully complete the task at hand.

9. **Stop procrastinating-** Set goals and deadlines, say no, and minimize distractions.

10. **Have fun**

    "Think of the times you've let self-doubt seep into your mind; the worry, the sleepless nights of thinking that you might not accomplish something, or wondering if you deserve that [fill in the blank] you been [hoping] for. Don't go there! Thoughts like that can only harm your emotional wellbeing. Being secure within yourself and who you are will only bring you prosperity in both your personal life and your career. Remind yourself that you are worthwhile, and you will find a new sense of confidence. If you can learn to value yourself and see your own worth, others around will see it too, and soon enough you'll be on the path to success!"

    -Motus Recruiting

CHAPTER 2
YOUR OOTD (OUTFIT OF THE DAY)

"Fashion is the armor to survive the reality of everyday life."
-Bill Cunningham

WHAT ARE YOU WEARING?

What is your OOTD? (a.k.a. Outfit Of The Day?) When working in the workplace, your dress attire must be appropriate professional, clean, neat, and comfortable. When you are working, the last thing that you want is to have your mind fixated on having to adjust your clothes while working. Practice sitting down and standing up multiple times to see how your clothes shift and adjust. Your goal is to be confident.

In a courtroom setting, do your research on the magistrate/judge you are assigned to, because you do not want to wear or do something that frustrates them.

They are human too, so they may have a pet peeve, and you want to have your best foot forward.

CLOTHING AND ACCESSORIES

Tops

- When wearing tops it is recommended to wear a bra, camisole, or tank top underneath.
- Avoid light color bras under light color tops. Please note: if you are wearing a white blouse even when you have a blazer on. When you take off your jacket you want to have a black, brown, or nude under garments (same applies for slips.)
- Your cleavage area, which is the bust line of your shirt, make sure you can easily button across the breast line. That way you do not have to worry about your shirt potentially coming loose.
- Make sure tops are appropriate length when tucked in. So, when you stand up your shirts are not coming out from your pants or skirt.

Sweaters/Jackets

- Wearing a blazer is highly recommended. Also, to be warn not only when cool temperatures but also recommended to cover arms and short sleeve shirts/blouses that are sleeveless.

Bottoms

- Pants to be appropriate length and hemmed at the bottom to prevent dragging pant legs.
- Pants with belt loops, wearing a belt is highly recommended.
- The pants that you wear make sure that the area across your crotch does not have the stretch wrinkles. Because at any given moment the thread can become unraveled. This is how you can tell if your pants are too tight in the back, if it is stretching cross the crotch in the front then it is too tight in the back too.
- Dresses/Skirts to be kneecap length, the slit to be a few inches, also recommend wearing a slip underneath. Latch the hook at the top. So, your dress/skirt does not unzip.

Clothing colors/patterns

- Avoid loud prints, super-bright colors. White, beige, pastels, nudes colors are ok.

- You want to have a visible aesthetic to the eye but not to the point that your words are being missed because people are too busy paying attention to your outfit.
- You want to feel good in what you are wearing you do not want to be a distraction to the work environment (the jury or to the judge).
- If you gain weight do not fear. Take your clothes to a consignment shop and swap it out for a bigger size same as if you lost weight.
- The goal is to be confident and to feel secure about what you have on because it comes through the way that you express yourself. It will definitely show that your mind is being fixated on adjusting your clothes.

Pantyhose/dress socks

- Recommended to wear.
- Pantyhose color not to be darker than the thread of your skirt.

Spanx
- Needs to be 8-10 hour friendly. Do not try to overdo it. If you want to give the hourglass appearance.

Shoes
- Dress shoes (loafers or flats) to be comfortable without holes, polished if possible.
- Shoes ½ an inch in a pump. Do not want to do a stiletto.
- Plain shades and colors.

Jewelry
- Wear at a minimal.
- Big blingy jewelry is not recommended.
- Earrings: Studs are best. Dangling earrings provides a distraction.

Belts
- Wear a belt, many females feel like they do not need to wear a belt. A pair of pants may feel snug but remember their going to rise and shift when they are sitting down standing up.

Eyeglasses/Contacts

- If you do not like to wear glasses get contacts and avoid very off shades of eye contacts.
- Sunglasses are not appropriate for inside the workplace.

HAIR AND MAKEUP

When it comes to hair and makeup in the workplace:

Hair: Make sure there is confidence in your hair too.

- To be presentable, clean.
- Avoid gaudy hair jewelry. When pining or clipping hair up.
- Carefully styled that compliments the professional vibe of your outfit.
- Must have a go to signature hair style even for bad hair days.

Makeup, it is best to keep the look polished, fabulous, and simple professional look using complementary colors.

- A nude color on the eyes with a section of color that matches the outfit.
- Avoid glamour make up, and looks. If heavy on the eye, must do soft on the lips and vice versa.

You do not want to look like you are going to audition.
- Apply blush just enough to highlight the cheekbones.
- A signature lipstick or light gloss, that compliments the skin tone.
- Bronzer- if want a dewy Sunkissed presentation.

Mirror talk

For help organizing an outfit, colors, styles, and patterns visit internet blogs, magazines, etc. Remember, always dress well, but keep it simple. Style is a way to say who you are without having to speak.

Unfortunately, criminal justice is a male-dominated world. You do not want to present yourself as eye candy. You want to be taken seriously for who you are. Males are going to look at your body and how you dress before they take you seriously. When you are in the workplace you want to walk in with the appearance you mean business, and that is the only reason you are there.

CHAPTER 3
CRIMINAL JUSTICE

Criminal justice, the career field that never sleeps. A field that genuinely shows great levels of servanthood, protection, and respect.

WORK-LIFE BALANCE

Working in criminal justice has some barriers for women and their success. Some positions with greater statutes and responsibilities (that equates to hectic work hours) can become hard to balance between work and her family. For women to succeed, it is important to have the support, strong mentorship, and professional perseverance.

WOMEN IN THE LAW

Let us take a look at history. 1869, was the year the National Woman's Suffrage Association was created in efforts to have the right for women to vote. The founders Susan B. Anthony and Elizabeth Cady Stanton, these bold women were heard, and the 19th Amendment was established, legalizing women's right to vote. At the time, women were secretaries to attorneys and police matrons. By the mid-1900s, there was an increase in women in law enforcement. In most fields of work, women went from social workers to active police officers. The International Association of Policewomen (IAWP) was founded by Alice Stebbins Wells in 1915.

In 1949, Burnita Shelton Matthews was the first woman US District Court Judge (which was 140 years after the Federal Court System was established). By the 1950s, the number of women on the force doubled. In 1968, two women in Indianapolis were on patrol duty.

Women police officers have brought new perspectives in handling conflict resolution strategies. How? Emotional intelligence and communication; women love communication along with being more emotional in nature than males.

In addition, communication is the key solution to many problems in policing. By communicating with offenders before actual physical enforcement, this strategy can better resolve conflicts. Four years later in 1972, police departments were prohibited of discriminating against women due to the expansion of the Civil Rights Act (Title VII of the 1964). Six years later, 10 % of corrections officers were women.

Sandra Day O'Connor served from 1981-2006 as the first woman United States Supreme Court Justice.

In the year of 1992, women graduated from law school as attorneys, making them qualified for higher judicial positions.

According to the National Women's Law Center: *"Approximately 30 percent of active United States district or trial court judges are women."*
- Janet Mulroney Clark, *"The Rise in Women Working in the Criminal Justice System."*

A year later Janet Reno became the first female U.S. Attorney General, serving eight years. The first minority to be Chief of Police of Atlanta, Georgia in 1994 was Beverly J. Harvard, who served eight years as well.

There are other positions in the criminal justice field that saw changes. In criminology, Freda Adler had the opportunity to be a consultant for the United Nations and became the president of the American Criminological Society.

In May of 2009, Sonia Sotomayor served as the first Hispanic and Latino Associate Justice on the Supreme Court.

November 2020 election, Kamala Harris, became the first Minority Vice President Elect.

Today only 36% on the 13-federal court of appeals sitting judges are female, and 33% of the US district court are female. Women as judges, magistrates, attorneys, and prosecutors can help bring a new perspective to many rulings.

WORKING IN CRIMINAL JUSTICE FIELD SYNOPSIS

The experience, the faces, and the emotions you will see, and you will learn many ways of procedures in the criminal justice field. The realization of how people live, what led to their situation, their emotions, or even the emotionlessness ways they cope can also be shocking. There are laws we are unfamiliar with until we step into the criminal justice field or unfortunately have a one-on-one involvement with a government official.

Learning how the judicial system works outside the classroom is different from what is depicted on television and movies. When any authoritarian position within the criminal justice field enforces a consequence, it will make changes to the lifestyle, for the better or worse of an individual (along with their family).

Like any job communication skills are important. Writing and using psychology in criminal justice is essential. Writing is connected to communicating with your colleagues, the public, the court officials, politicians, and even in the news. When it comes to psychology, the course will be your precious asset for you. Psychology provides the underlying knowledge of what, and why people do what they do.

Along with serving as an aid to help understand if there is a connection to mental health and the crime committed or if the act was committed out of desperation. With the use of psychology, can reveal the next steps, that a criminal may do along with preparing to put tactics in place to protect yourself and colleagues when de-escalating a conflict.

There are good reasons to work in this field, due to job stability. Unfortunately, there will always be crime. Therefore, workers are needed and there are many career options to choose from. Some of these options intersect. Intelligence is another reason one may choose to work in this field.

One could choose to work in this field because of a need to respond quickly to the challenges criminals are involved in, along with de-escalating the situations in a healthy and safe manner.

The health care and retirement benefits check out across the board. From life insurance, student loan repayment programs, to tuition assistance, and training assistance, there are many wonderful benefits. If you are a federal worker, you will also be taken care of beneficially. Another key factor to consider is that working in this field makes it possible to retire early. Some chose to retire early and work in another field or continue in criminal justice related departments.

THE THREE COMPONENTS

There are three components that work to prevent and punish crime: the law enforcement, court system, and the corrections system.

Law enforcement includes police and investigators who help prevent crimes in the communities by the way of arresting.

This makes law enforcement the very first group of authority that will encounter a criminal in the criminal justice system.

The second, after an arrest and jail experience, is the court system where the criminal becomes the defendant who will come before the court, with the opportunity to defend themselves. "All rise all rise the honorable judge, presiding," will echo in the courtroom. The court system includes the judge, attorneys, prosecutors, witnesses, jailers, stenographer, jurors, and other needed court personnel. Some cases are dismissed due to lack of evidence, or a motion to suppress evidence. There is an estimate of over 94 percent of state cases which result in plea bargains.

Lastly, there is the correctional system. Depending on the outcome of the court's ruling, the defendant will be sentenced to prison or probation. If the ruling is probation, the defendant will remain in the community instead of receiving a jail sentence and will be required to report to probation officers regularly. For incarceration, the defendant is bound to the corrections system, the prison wardens, and the correction officers of the state until the defendant's full sentence is served or shortened by decision of the judge.

WHAT AREA OF CRIMINAL JUSTICE INTEREST YOU?

There are many areas of criminal justice. The criminal justice system has various government entities. The top popular areas are: Police officer/Sheriff, Private Investigator, Judge/Magistrate, Adult/Juvenile Probation Officer, Parole Officer, Bailiff, Court Administrator, Court Reporter, Paralegal, Secret Service Agent, CIA Analyst, FBI Agent, Crime scene Investigator, Security officer, Victims Advocate, Social Worker, Prison Psychologist, and US Park Police.

The above areas require a high school diploma and sometimes a bachelor's degree. For a selective area of concentration, a master's degree is required. One thing to remember is there will always be crime, therefore, (unfortunately) therefore there will always be a need for a position in the criminal justice field and a way to move up the ranks.

THE CAMPAIGN TRAIL

Many candidates in the criminal justice field at some time will have to run for office to either keep their seat in office or seek a new role/office seat. These are police/sheriff's, magistrates/judges, mayor, governor etc.

Working on a campaign is the greatest opportunity to gain leadership skills, demanding high level of motivation, working with a team of different backgrounds and skill sets. Another perk of the possibility of meeting a celebrity.

Campaign life is different, and not for everyone. Walking parades, endless nights of planning, fast pace environment, phone's buzzing, ringing, campaign parties, lots of money and business cards exchanging. One thing to remember the person and side you represent, that associating will follow you for better or for worse. Make sure you are at peace within with who you are representing. What they stand for, who they are and what they are promising. This also represents who you are as a person as well.

CRIMINAL JUSTICE FINAL THOUGHT

I can tell you from my personal experience that I understand these facts about this field may be a little overwhelming. However, do not be intimidated. This position helps you be a better person from within by building your confidence, self-esteem, and developing quick troubleshooting skills. Defendants, prisoners, even court representatives will test your buttons however, another key factor is be consistent. Be consistent in your talk, and your actions. That way, if someone attempts to lie on you the courtroom, the jailers, and your supervisor will know that whatever someone presents to them about you is false due to the fact they know how moral and consistent you are. This saved me in certain situations and I still was employed and not behind bars.

Working in the justice center, there was never a dull moment. Day by day there are many people that are waiting in long lines and in desperate need of being served; whether it is having their case file pulled, rap sheet printed, or search of their additional case files etc. Remember the people you will encounter you do not know, those who are waiting to be served, are not your friends. It is so easy to get caught in a bad situation due to associating yourself with someone you really do not know. They could easily make up something to the judge on record mentioning you. As I mentioned earlier, being consistent and ethical can save you from situations, so be careful. Simply because that individual is there almost as much as you are, that is not necessarily a good thing. Yes, some individuals come to court for good reasons, to dispute or pay a ticket, to file a motion, a wedding or for moral support. However, you do not fully know a person in passing or after having a two-minute conversation. This fact can cause the need to listen to your gut and instincts in knowing what you share with them about yourself, along with being aware of your surroundings.

HISTORY POINTS OF THE CRIMINAL JUSTICE SYSTEM

The criminal justice system was created during the Revolutionary War (also known as the American Revolution) by the British from 1775-1783.

The reason for creating the system was to help justify the government's punishment of their citizens. This is where the titles "magistrates" and "judges" originated.

In the year of 1787, the United States Constitution was signed with the understanding that this was a way to safeguard specific freedoms and rights of citizens, by limiting the powers of the government in a way to prevent oppression. The forming of the amendments to the Constitution followed, which included the first five (also known as the Bill of Rights) and was focused on the police and courts.

- The Fourth Amendment (unreasonable searches and seizures) is the reason why law enforcement is required to obtain a warrant.
- The Fifth Amendment (due process) means an individual cannot be held to answer for a crime that would deprive the individual of their freedom, property, and life. During arrests, the law enforcement officer is required to read the Miranda Rights.
- The Sixth Amendment states, after the individual becomes a defendant, law enforcement is required to

provide all information in their case of charges against the individual. Therefore, all charges are to be known to the defendant(s) and to attorney(s). The Sixth Amendment also provides the assurance to defendants of a speedy and public trial before an unbiased jury.

- The Seventh Amendment provides the right to the defendant to a jury trial in civil cases.
- Lastly, the Eighth Amendment was formed to focus on the courts to prohibit the use of excessive bail, fines, or any other decision(s) that would result in a cruel and unusual way of punishment.

After the establishment of the Constitution, Congress created district courts, which would operate under the Judiciary Act of 1789; thus, dividing the country into thirteen judicial districts. Three circuits were created in the thirteen districts: one overseeing the eastern part of the nation, one overseeing the middle part of the nation and one overseeing the southern part of the nation.

In 1790, "all rise, all rise," echoed in the courtroom as the U.S. Supreme Court was in session and became America's most important place of decision making in the nation. The number of judges in the U.S. Supreme Court was nine, serving 16 years. Today, judges serve for life.

The court system on the Federal level includes: The Supreme Court, Court of Appeals, District Court and Special Court. The court system on the state level includes: State Supreme Court, County Court, Municipal Court, and possibly the Mayor's Court.

Call in the enforcements to their posts. The term "watchman" was used during the Colonial Era to identify law enforcement personnel, Peace Officers, and Sheriffs, whose job was to interrupt and prevent crimes, collect taxes within the town, and receive special pay for servicing warrants.

A change occurred in Philadelphia, PA in 1833; the decision to have day policing as well as watchmen on patrol. Philadelphia became the first city to conduct 24-hour policing, which, after a decade, created police departments across America.

In the early 1900s, America saw the implementation of jails, prisons, and the imposing of fines to align with criminal offenses, however, many could not pay. With the growth in corrections, the prisons were creating tactics for managing inmates. The hopes were the inmate would reflect on what they had done and would choose to be a better person, not allowing crime to be their way of life. The correction officers would enforce periods of isolation, cell time, recreation/work duty, and visitation rules.

Here comes the FBI! The FBI agents were recruited from the police department. In the 1908 quest to create a detective force, members of the police department were recruited and reported to the Department of Justice. Five years later, there was the creation of the federal income tax, which resulted in tax fraud investigations. Criminal activity cases began to rise, such as women prostitution across state lines, as well as stolen vehicles taken across state lines.

During the 1920s there was an increase in cases that violated state and federal laws, (organized crime and liquor violations) that required frequent use of wiretapping and searches. Also, there was a demand for more prisons, which included the building of the first federal women's prison in West Virginia, opening in 1927. The judge said it was similar to a fashionable boarding school.

The role of the FBI expanded to counterintelligence and counter terrorism with a breakthrough year in 1923. The law enforcement component of the criminal justice system had expanded with the first crime labs in France, and the United States. There was a crime lab located in Los Angeles as well as a police school. More innovations included the use of patrol vehicles and new investigative and technology procedures, including fingerprinting, filing, and handwriting systems.

With all the police patrolling and multiple locations of police departments being built around the nations, reports surfaced of corruption within the police force and not enough efforts being done to help inmates with rehabilitation. Officials recognized the need of a better sense of professionalism in the different levels (federal, state, and local).

Crime rates escalated, which sparked the need for a new program to provide nationwide statistics on certain growing crimes – the UCR (Uniform Crime Reporting Program). The program would help provide precise data on crime trends in the nation.

The crimes included statistics on aggravated assault, arson, burglary, larceny (theft of property), manslaughter/murder, motor vehicle theft, rape, and robbery.

There was not a statistic of increased movement in transportation during the Great Depression. People were traveling to different states and law enforcement could not monitor. Law enforcement knew action must take place quickly on a federal level.

After a kidnapping and murder, the Lindbergh Act of 1932 was enforced, meaning if someone is taken against their will across the state, this would be deemed as a federal crime. Over the years, specific crimes have continued to grow white-collar crimes, drug cases and organized crime. When citizens needed to call for help, the only choices were to call the police department or be connected to the operator. Neighborhoods began creating neighborhood watches to have more eyes and ears on suspicious activity within their neighborhoods. In 1957, the National Association of Fire Chiefs recommended having one number that citizens could use in case of emergencies. Congress realized that crime had shifted the sense of quality of life and culture in the United States and enforced, in 1967, the Crime Control and Safe Streets Act. Year later, the United States presented to the nation a simple set of numbers that would "be easy to remember and quick to dial." The number was 9-1-1. The first emergency call was in the state of Alabama. Police wanted to reconnect with the community, so they began patrolling by foot and riding horseback throughout their areas.

The Civil Rights Act had been signed into law (1964). This new law declared it illegal to discriminating against nationality origin, race, and gender. The law also declared illegal of segregation Jim Crow Laws, Voting Rights Act, and Indian Civil Act. The Age Discrimination in Employment Act was passed by Congress to keep all older workers from discrimination issues in the workplace.

Within 1965-1980 The population of the prison has exploded, Judges have ordered longer mandatory sentences, drug cases, prisoners in need of rehabilitation, the cost of building more prisons and operating national prisons, which is the highest in history.

In the prisons, the inmates were able to work manufacturing jobs for the military, public roads, and they learned new skill trades. Outside the prisons, local businesses nearby protested by claiming an unfair competition. Along with labor unions protesting that the inmates are being receiving low wages.

Prison inmates received alternative assistance from outside the prison walls in an effort to lower costs to the prisons. Outside corporations were granted the opportunity to provide facilities, under the order of the state, to provide drug treatment centers and halfway houses to inmates.

Technology made a transition into the nation as well during this time frame, providing convenience to the way citizens lived, and providing new ways for crimes to be committed. Law enforcement needed to keep up with the changes technology had set. The internet, cell phones, other electronic devices and network communications made everyone concerned about privacy and identity theft, due to technology connections.

New laws were created such as copyright, and trademarks. Today the ongoing issue in the criminal justice system is the internet and how easy it is used across state and national lines. The government created a Computer Fraud and Abuse Act that was used for another reason, but now it has focused on monitoring the information over the internet.

At the end of the 1900s, crime statistics were 35 million, and the number of victims was about 2.3 million.

The nationwide fear caused the gun purchases to increase, so did the demand for security systems. With the rapid availability of technology connections, crime has become more public, and people have never feared living in a common place because the frequency of crime. A pivotal time in history has kept fear on the minds of many, the mass shootings, the change, and enhanced security at airports, malls, public buildings, etc. have been an understanding of each day a change in some sector will take place and citizens will have to learn how to adjust to the impact it would affect in their lives.

The new millennium!

In the year 2000, the Department of Justice Criminal Division marked their 100th anniversary. There was the formation of the Department of Homeland Security, and funding granted for the use of DNA technology for criminal justice procedures regarding the rights of convicted felons. There was also the creation of the Gang Unit, and the U.S. Supreme court forbidding the death penalty for juveniles. In addition, the first Hispanic woman was appointed to the Supreme Court. By the end of 2011, about seven million people were on parole.

Certain states were approved to house inmates in private prisons but decided to prohibit future agreement contracts.

By 2019, the main issues of concern were the drug crime policy, human trafficking, cannabis, mental health needs in the criminal justice system, law enforcement, civil and constitutional issues, child support and incarcerated parents, and stand your ground in self-defense.

As the year 2020 unfolds, crime will always be, but what part of the criminal justice system will you work in? What will your story be of how you decided to work in the field?

CHAPTER 4
APPLY!

"If one advances confidently in the direction of his dreams, and endeavors to live the life which he has imagined, he will meet with a success unexpected in common hours."
-Henry David Thoreau

ROLES AND RESPONSIBILITIES

Like every job, there are roles and responsibilities. Dress and appropriate attire, behavior, and professionalism are always key. There is an understanding that being an intern or working in the field there are rules and procedures to abide by.

Obeying the rules and following these rules will not only ensure your safety but also ensure that others are working safely. Being on time and attending meetings (being prepared for meetings with a notepad, pen, or pencil) communicating and listening, being an observer, asking questions, being respectful, participating in group participation, and show initiative. You must also report to your supervisor about conflicts, inappropriate conduct, or any wrongdoings. Remember there are always requirements to work in a healthy and safe environment.

APPLY FOR THE POSITION

Apply! Apply! How you get in will also determine how far you go. It is usually who you know. Criminal justice does tend to be political as well, so keep that in mind. Also, if you were volunteering on a campaign trail do not have any skeletons in your closet. Whom you talk to, and who you involve yourself with matters. People are always watching and taking notes. It could affect your job and your future simply by association, so do be mindful of that. It is sad but true.

One thing I personally would had rethought was to apply outside of the city that I live in. Due to the constant involvement of defendants in the area living their lives outside of court/correctional facilities, such as the halfway houses. By living in the city area defendants live in, will have a higher chance of running into them at stores etc. Likeliness of defendants would want to discuss their case outside the court walls.

INTERNSHIP VS FIELD EXPERIENCE

Internships are hands-on experience to gain opportunities in an established business for the intern to prove their skills from their classroom teaching to the real world. The internship positions are at an entry-level and are required for credits to graduate. An internship usually involves more time in one-on-one and responsibilities. The only difference between an internship and the field is the field experience is not credited towards graduation.

Applicants are required to be junior or senior status. There are two different paths: 1. Corrections 2. Law enforcement track. Contact your college professor or someone in the criminal justice field you desire to work in.

CHAPTER 5
EVALUATION

"We should always be ready to explore our positive and negative traits by evaluating our real self from time to time."
-Dr Prem Jagyasi

EVALUATIONS

Evaluations are essential to the place of employment and the employees. The purpose of evaluations is to identify the areas of your ability in different roles of responsibilities, goals, and accomplishments. Each area of ranking will be Exceeds Expectations, areas that Meet Expectations, Improvements needed, and Does Not Meet Expectations. Evaluations also help learn where and how to expand your skillset as well as a determination of a promotion or a raise. Evaluations are judged based on the overall performance, not a single incident good nor bad.

EVALUATION FACTORS

Based on Employee Appraisal Form. Some evaluation factors that are evaluated are:

Academic knowledge: Displays the academic knowledge in ways to contribute to the workplace.

Written and Oral Communications: Communicate clearly and intelligently in person and during phone and email contact.

Dedication: Reports to work on time and uses time constructively.

Cooperation: Willingly accepts work assignments as well as willing accepts changes in assignments not directly related to job.

Initiative: Performs assigned duties with little or no supervision, even under pressure. Strives to meet deadlines and seek supervisor's approval when necessary.

Performance: Good working knowledge of job assignments. Organizes and performs work in a timely, professional manner.

Analysis and Judgment: Ability to analyze and discern facts, solving problems, and making sound decisions.

Character: Accepts constructive criticism without unfavorable responses. Displays self-confidence and maturity.

Responsiveness: Handles stressful situations with tact.

Personality: Demonstrates a pleasant, calm personality when dealing with customers and fellow employees.

Work Habits: Maintains neat and orderly workstation and paperwork.

Teamwork: Works well with fellow employees without friction.

Appearance: Well groomed. Clean. Neat. Dresses appropriately for work.

CHAPTER 6
STAY ALERT

This is a reminder that while working in criminal justice as a female, you will encounter many different races, genders, unstable minds, people suffering from trauma, anger, loneliness, etc. Within any justice center, you are in an elevator, stairway, or hallway, and there will be individuals from the community there. This being said, people are always watching. As a female we must always be aware of our surroundings, listen to our gut, stay calm, think smart, have small talk, and get help when we need to.

LISTEN TO YOUR GUT

Our gut instincts will give us good confirmation on a matter. Listen, trust your gut! Do not make yourself vulnerable. I worked in the courthouse for 5 years and experienced many things and had many moments were my gut instincts began speaking to me in a way that cautioned me to be alert.

During the first week of my internship, I sat on a hallway bench one morning while waiting for the judge's chambers to be unlocked. A gentleman came and sat on the bench next to me. He asked if I was an attorney and I replied no. He then begins to tell me about his case and his felony offense, and as he talked, I became extremely uncomfortable. I started having an instinctual feeling, like something in my gut was off. It was so strong, I got up and waited on another floor of the courthouse.

BE AWARE OF YOUR SURROUNDINGS

Awareness is mandatory. Always be observant and call for help immediately; your life counts on it.

When you know your surroundings, you will be able to quickly notice things that are out of the ordinary and be able to take appropriate actions if need be. One action in particular may be to call the police or a supervisor.

Tips to remember:

1. Do not be predictable.
2. Take a different route to and from work.
3. Leave a little earlier or/and leave a little later.
4. Watch yourself when you would be most vulnerable. (like a bathroom down the hall in a corner)
5. Go to your store, bank, laundromat etc. on different days.
6. Switch it up; go to a different store, bank, or laundromat.
7. Do not think that the changes around you are innocent or fine. Do not let your guard down.
8. Trust your gut instincts.
9. If you are at a location and you do not feel safe leaving, ask for someone to escort you out to until you feel safe.

Each day at the courthouse, I made sure I was aware of my surroundings. I frequently took the quiet stairways and elevators. Yes, I had a work phone, but it was always my responsibility to be aware of my surroundings and to be consistent in my actions.

One day I was in one of the courtrooms preparing for court to begin. I began addressing the rules of the court, and one rule specifically mentions there is no use of cellphones.

As I walked through the courtroom, a gentleman had his phone up following me as I moved around the room. He was recording or taking pictures of me. I told him to remove footage and verified. This incident heightened my level of alertness and awareness. All the kidnapping and trafficking going on in this world, who knows who he could have shared the footage with? So, beware of someone frequently being overly observant of you.

A friend of mine asked me to speak to a college student who started a job in an adult probation department. I informed her to be aware of her surroundings since she was working closely with defendants with felonies (high degree cases of drugs, theft, rape, and murder). I also informed her to be aware of her dress attire, and to also have two to three friends whom she could call to check in with, and who could come pick her up in case of an immediate need or emergency. We discussed changing her walking and driving route from work every now and then and to have small talk but not to reveal much about herself for protection. I advised her to never reveal where she lives and her family's identities. Months later, she informed me that she had incident. A man had been watching her and followed her. She made a phone call to a friend and was able to remain safe. She thanked me for giving her the tips. Again, be aware of your surroundings, think smart, and act quickly.

I even turned down a promotion at a different job due to not feeling safe in the building where I would be working. Your wellbeing and safety are more important than anything else.

STAY CALM, THINK SMART, SMALL TALK
Stay calm and do not be intimidated by the people in the community. Think smart. Your life is connected to your decisions so make smart decisions. Provide small talk. Protect your reputation, your identity, and your family.

There were times when I was out in the community handling personal responsibilities where a defendant from one of the courts rooms, I worked in approached me. They stated "went to court and I got charged for..." I had to inform them they are not to speak with me regarding their case and to call or report to the court, not me. I mentioned this due to the fact that you can never give people an opportunity to lie on you. There is a possibility they could make a statement to the court that I had instructed them to do or say something and basically put words in my mouth.

Earlier in the beginning of this book, I emphasized that consistency is important. Being consistent in your working habits (what you say and do) so your supervisor will know this is not your character, will save you from any persecution and reputation.

KEEP YOUR INFORMATION PRIVATE

Everyone does not need to know your business. Where you live, where you shop, your phone number, your family, and romantic life, etc. are private and should remain that way. The less you share, the better you are protecting yourself from predators, gossip, and anyone who may attempt to attack or violate you in any way.

CHAPTER 7
GETTING HELP

In the end, you always have to protect yourself.

PROTECTION ORDER

As mentioned in the chapter before, obtaining a protection order is an option available if needed. There are three different types of protection orders. Temporary, Civil, and an Anti-Stalking Civil Protection Order. These can be filed in any city. It usually takes 24 hours to get a protection order. Protection Orders protects you if someone is stalking, psychically assaulted, sexually assaulted, or threatened you or your immediate circle. A judge grants an order of protection. There is no cost and no need for an attorney, but you can talk to an attorney at your discretion. You will also need to go to a hearing. For assistance reach out to Domestic Violence Unit, Victim Assistance Program, and a police officer.

See the Appendix on information regarding a Protection Order

POLICE REPORT

To file a police officer report, visit a police station. In some areas, you can file a police report online. Again, if you or someone is in immediate danger call 911 immediately.

Information needed:

1. Time
2. Date
3. Location
4. Your name and ID number
5. Names of other people that were present
6. Your contact and witness' contact information
7. A thorough description of the incident
8. What brought you to the scene
9. What happened when you arrived?

FINAL NOTE

Congratulations! You have finished the book! I hope this book opened your eyes, and heart about not just the tips of working in the criminal justice field, but also confidence, mindset, apparel, self-awareness, and oh yes, lipstick! This book has discussed different criminal justice fields that are available, tips on the clothing selection, working with supervisors and coworkers, how important your mindset is, the connection of confidence within, and having an awareness of your surroundings along with reaching out for help. Now take this new information and put it in motion.

I suggest visiting and taking free personality tests that will help with working with coworkers, friends, and other loved ones, work towards understanding yourself on a deeper level. **The Four temperaments Test.** https:/temperaments.fighunter.com/ Temperaments are focused on how we deal with emotions and thoughts. It helps reveal how we work with others.

The Myers–Briggs test.

https://www.16personalities.com/free-personality-test

This is a popular personality test that originated in the mid-1950s to help women find what career was best for them. It was a recruitment promotional tool. Today it is popular and continues to be used in businesses, and academics.

Do not be afraid to take self-defense classes, active shooter classes, conflict management courses and First Aid/CPR/AED training. Classes and trainings help expand your skillset and help boost your confidence.

I hope this book has been informative and worth note-taking. Thank you for reading! Be safe!

THE AUTHOR'S CRIMINAL JUSTICE EXPERIENCE

DeNaye' Dotson is an optimistic woman of God, who has the willingness to work hard and pursue her dreams. She has an eye for creativity, a heart of ministry servanthood, a joyful personality, and a strong determination to succeed in life.

When it came to career, DeNaye' and her best friend decided to work together in the career field of Criminal Justice. Her best friend longed to be a judge and DeNaye' decided to be her bailiff. Both attended colleges, but after a few semesters, their life goals changed.

DeNaye' graduated with a Paralegal Degree in 2008 from the University of Akron in Akron, Oh, which led to a hands-on experience journey in the field of Criminal Justice. After completing an internship working in a courthouse, she gained a village of seasoned, authoritative, sharp minded colleagues and friends. The opportunity opened for DeNaye' to assist the Court Administration, Judges, Magistrates, Bailiffs, and

Probation Officers. There was never a dull moment in the building; every day was something new!

DeNaye' transitioned to another branch of criminal justice into the heart of working in the admissions department of a Community Corrections and Chemical Dependency Treatment Agency. Part of the position was to transport inmates from prison to halfway houses. This required background clearance from the Ohio Department of Rehabilitation and Corrections. Some of the responsibilities included walking into the prisons, signing for the agency's client to be released and transported by van to a halfway house.

DeNaye' could not believe she was doing such a service to the community in this way. On the ride from the prison(s) the person went from an inmate number to a client. Hearing their stories, while driving DeNaye' reflected on how we take things for granted. Some clients were scared to be on the other side of the prison walls, since prison was all they knew. Others thought they may die quicker than in prison due to the fear of people in community, and random shootings. Some hoped they would not be car/motion sick, others were excited to prove to the courts they had learned their lessons, and a client even stood amazed the toilets in the rest stop flushed on their own!

DeNaye' would travel the highways several times a month pick up clients from prison and transport them to different halfway homes. She would see some of the clients she had dropped off with big smiles and wave each time. It was good to see they were still on the right path and not being sent back to prison.

Today, DeNaye' continues to serve the community as a State of Ohio Notary, Administrative Assistant, trainer, author, painter and an entrepreneur.

Connect with DeNaye' at DeNayeDotson.com

APPENDIX

Protection order Frequent Asked Question

1. **Can I get an Order of Protection?**

You can ask for an Order of Protection if the person abusing you or threatening you is a family member, intimate partner, or former intimate partner. You can also ask for an Order of Protection if someone is stalking you, has sexually assaulted you, or has assaulted you, whether or not you have had an intimate relationship with that person.

2. **I think I want an Order of Protection. What do I do first?**

First, please talk to a victim advocate. A victim advocate can help you decide if an Order of Protection is right for you. Sometimes an Order of Protection would not be in your best interest. An advocate can help you figure out if an Order of Protection would help you or not. S/he can also give you more information about how to apply for an Order of Protection.

3. What do I do next?

You file a petition for an Order of Protection in court. There is no cost. You have to sign an affidavit about what your abuser has done to you. An affidavit is a form that you swear is true and sign in front of a notary or a Judge. If the court finds you are in danger of harm, you will first get a Temporary Order of Protection. Then a hearing will be set. You must attend the hearing if you want the Temporary Order of Protection to stay in place. Your abuser can attend the hearing, too. S/he can tell his or her side of the story to the judge. At the hearing, the judge will decide if you should have an Order of Protection. An Order of Protection can last a few days, months, years, or be permanent.

4. Where do I file an Order of Protection?

A petition for Order of Protection can be filed in city, justice, or district court. If you and the other party have a family law case happening in district court, the petition must be filed in district court. A family law case includes dissolution and parenting plans.

5. **Do I need an attorney?**

You do not need an attorney to get an Order of Protection. But it may help you to talk to an attorney before you file a petition for an Order of Protection. It may help you to talk to an attorney before your hearing or to have an attorney help you at the hearing. **You may choose to represent yourself. If you ask a court to grant you an Order of Protection, the following information will help you understand the hearing process and preset your case effectively.**

6. **Do I have to go to the hearing?**

Yes. If you are the Petitioner and do not attend the hearing, the court will dismiss your case, which means that you will not receive an Order of Protection.

7. **What if I cannot attend?**

If you absolutely cannot attend the hearing because of an important reason (such as sickness, job interview, family emergency, etc.), you should call the court in which your hearing is set and ask that the hearing be rescheduled. Some courts may require you to file a document called a "motion for continuance".

8. **How do I prepare for the hearing?**

Decide the relief you want the court to give you. You will be asking the judge to grant you an Order of Protection against the person who abused you or threatened to abuse you. You need to tell the judge specifically what you want the Order to say. You can ask the judge to: Order the Respondent not to hurt you; Order the Respondent not to harass or otherwise disturb you (and/or your children); Order the Respondent not to contact you (in person, through 3rd parties, through writing, by email, by telephone, etc.); Order the Respondent to stay a specific distance from you, your residence and/or your place of employment; Order the Respondent to vacate the home you are living in; Order the Respondent to allow you access to your personal property; Order the Respondent not to possess a gun or other dangerous weapon; Order the Respondent to attend batterer's intervention counseling or drug/alcohol counseling.

9. **Decide the evidence you want to use.**

Evidence is what you present in court to prove that the Respondent has harmed or may harm you (and/or your child). Evidence can be your testimony, the testimony of witnesses, documents, photos, or objects such as torn clothing or a weapon.

10. What happens at the hearing?

If the Respondent does not appear at the hearing, the judge may grant an Order of Protection for you without considering any evidence or may require you to present your evidence so that s/he has it on the record. It is likely (but not guaranteed) that if the Respondent does not appear, you will be granted an Order of Protection. If the Respondent appears and agrees that an Order of

Protection should be granted; the judge will probably grant one for you.

Your Case

If the Respondent appears and disagrees that an Order of Protection be granted, the judge will probably ask you to present your case (your side of the story) first.

This includes:
1. Being sworn in to testify truthfully.
2. Taking the witness stand.
3. Presenting your evidence.
4. Asking for the specific relief you need.

The judge may ask you specific questions about the situation. After you have finished, the Respondent will have a chance to ask you questions. After the Respondent has finished asking you questions, you will have the opportunity to ask questions of your witnesses. After each of your witnesses is done testifying, the Respondent has the opportunity to ask them questions.

Evidence for Petitioners

"Evidence" is what you present in court to prove that the respondent has harmed or may harm you (and/or your child). Evidence can be your statements (called "testimony"), documents, photos, or objects such as torn clothing or a weapon. The following are examples of the types of evidence that can be used to show the judge that you are in danger and need an Order of Protection.

Your Testimony

You should tell the judge why you want the Order of Protection, including why you are afraid of the respondent. You should include information about times when the respondent abused you. If there have been many abusive times, you should focus your testimony on the most recent and the worst. Describe each time you were abused by telling "who, how, when and where".

You can tell the judge about:

Abuse, threats of abuse, past protective orders, violence against others and animals. Testimony of Witnesses, Physical Items

How can I make sure the judge considers my evidence?
The judge will consider the evidence that s/he is allowed to consider based on the law. It is likely that the Respondent (or his attorney) will "object" to some of your evidence. If that happens, don't worry - just be prepared to explain to the judge why you think the evidence should be considered.

Respondent's Case
After you have presented your side of the story, the judge will allow the Respondent to present his/her evidence, including having his/her witnesses testify. If you disagree with what the Respondent or witnesses say, don't interrupt. You will have a chance to ask the Respondent questions after he/she has testified. You will also have a chance to ask witnesses questions after each has testified and you can use those opportunities to show that the evidence you disagree with is either false or taken out of context. You also will be given the opportunity to testify in response to issues the Respondent brings up

that you did not discuss while you presented your case. After both you and the Respondent have finished presenting your cases, the Judge will make a decision as to whether or not to grant an Order of Protection for you.

What if my abuser violates the order of protection?
Violation of an Order of Protection is a crime. You should call local law enforcement immediately. The abuser may be arrested. You should also keep a written diary of all the times the abuser violates the Order of Protection. It could help law enforcement and the prosecutor file criminal charges against the abuser. Only the respondent (or abuser) under an Order of Protection may be cited for a violation; the petitioner (you) who filed for the order may not be cited. A violation of any terms of an Order of Protection is punishable.

How do I protect myself at court?
Sit far away from the abuser. Bring a friend, relative, or a Crime Victim Advocate with you. Ask the judge to keep the abuser there for several minutes when court is over and leave quickly. If you think the abuser is following you when you leave, call the police immediately.

How do I protect myself at home?

Learn places where you can get help. Keep a phone in a room you can lock from the inside. Get a cellular phone that you keep with you at all times. Plan an escape route out of your home to a safe place. Teach it to your children. Set up a plan with your neighbors to signal them when you need them to call the police. Pack a bag with important things. Keep it ready in case you have to leave quickly. Put it in a safe place or give it to someone you trust. Make sure the bag has cash, keys, court papers, passports, birth certificates, medical records, medicines, formula, diapers. Take a self-defense course. If your abuser has moved out: Change the locks on doors and windows. Ask neighbors to call police if they see the abuser at your house. Get an unlisted phone number.

What if I am threatened or attacked in my home?

Stay away from the kitchen, where the abuser can find weapons like knives. Stay away from small spaces such as bathrooms, closets. Call 911. Get to a room with a door or window. Lock the abuser out if you can. Run to a neighbor or a public place.

How can I help my children be safe?

Teach them to not get in the middle of a fight, even if they want to help. Teach them how to get to safety, call emergency numbers, and give your address and phone number to police. Give the school/daycare a copy of your Protection Order. Tell them not to release your children to anyone without talking to you first. Use a password so they know it's you on the phone. Give them a photo of your abuser. Make sure the children know who to tell at school if they see the abuser. Make sure the school will not give out your address or phone number.

What are other ways I can protect myself?

Change your regular travel habits. Get rides with people. Bank and shop at different places. Cancel bank accounts or credit cards you shared with the abuser and open new ones. Keep a cell phone. Program it to speed-dial emergency numbers. Keep your Order of Protection with you always. It is valid in all states.

How can I protect myself at work?

Keep your Order of Protection with you. Give a picture of your abuser to coworkers and security guards. Tell your supervisors about your abuser. Ask them to help you. Don't go out alone. Ask a security guard or coworker to walk you to your car or bus. If your abuser contacts you at work, save the voice mail or email and tell your supervisor.

The information above can also be viewed on: https://dojmt.gov/wp-content/uploads/OVS-Getting-an-Order-of-Protection.pdf

REFERENCES

"5 Influential Women in The History of Criminal Justice." *South University*, www.southuniversity.edu/news-and-blogs/2013/03/5-influential-women-in-the-history-of-criminal-justice.

"5 Things You Should Know Before Enrolling in a Criminal Justice Master's Program." *Online.sju*, 23 Feb. 2020, online.sju.edu/graduate/masters-criminal-justice/resources/articles/5-things-you-should-know-before-enrolling-in-a-criminal-justice-masters-program.

"10 Events In Criminal Justice History That Changed Law Enforcement Forever." www.copsplus.com/resource-10-important-events-changed-law-enforcement.

"A Quote by Prem Jagyasi." *Goodreads*, Goodreads, www.goodreads.com/quotes/9699553-we-should-always-be-ready-to-explore-our-positive-and.

Austin, Julia. "Negative Phrases You Need To Stop Saying." *MadameNoire*, MadameNoire, 28 Mar. 2020, madamenoire.com/1065298/negative-phrases-you-need-to-stop-saying/.

"Bill Cunningham Quotes (Author of Fashion Climbing)." *Goodreads*, Goodreads, www.goodreads.com/author/quotes/15401305.Bill_Cunningham.

Burgess, Beth. "10 Tips To Boost Your Confidence At Work." *Lifehack*, Lifehack, 17 Mar. 2014, www.lifehack.org/articles/productivity/10-tips-for-boosting-your-confidence-work.html.

Clark, Janet Mulroney. "The Rise in Women Working in the Criminal Justice System." *Work*, 21 Nov. 2017, work.chron.com/rise-women-working-criminal-justice-system-25864.html.

"Confidence." *Psychology Today*, Sussex Publishers, www.psychologytoday.com/us/basics/confidence.

Clear, James. "The Science of Developing Mental Toughness in Health, Work, and Life." *James Clear*, 4 Feb. 2020, jamesclear.com/mental-toughness.

"Criminal Justice." *Wikipedia*, Wikimedia Foundation, 15 May 2020, en.wikipedia.org/wiki/Criminal_justice.

Eat, Pray, Love. Dir. Ryan Murphy. Columbia Pictures, 2010. Film

"DeNaye'" Picture. DeNaye's Cellphone. 2012.

"FREE 7 Sample Performance Evaluation Forms in PDF: MS Word." *FREE 7 Sample Performance Evaluation Forms in PDF | MS Word*, www.sampletemplates.com/business-templates/performance-evaluation-form.html.

Gillis, Kariann. "The Importance of Confidence in the Workplace." *Motus Recruiting*, 6 June 2018, motusrecruiting.com/the-importance-of-confidence-in-the-workplace/.

"Henry David Thoreau Quotes." *BrainyQuote*, Xplore, www.brainyquote.com/quotes/henry_david_thoreau_163655.

"Interesting Facts and Tips about Lipstick." *Facts about Lipstick - Useful Tips and Interesting Facts*, www.lipstickhistory.com/lipstick-facts/interesting-facts-about-lipstick.

"Jail Image." *Jail Free Image at CLKER.com*, 31 2016, http://www.clker.com/clipart-411312.html.

"Mental Toughness and Perceived Stress in Police and Fire Officers." *Policing: An International Journal*, www.emerald.com/insight/content/doi/10.1108/PIJPSM-01-2017-0013/full/html.

MinisterSnow4423. *Evaluation.docx - EMPLOYEE APPRAISAL FORM Employee Employee ID Position Date of Last Evaluation Dedication Performance Cooperation Initiative*. 10 Sept. 2018, www.coursehero.com/file/32988741/evaluationdocx/.

"Modern Criminal Justice." *Crime and Punishment in America Reference Library*, Encyclopedia.com, 23 May 2020, www.encyclopedia.com/law/encyclopedias-almanacs-transcripts-and-maps/modern-criminal-justice.

MONTANA DEPARTMENT OF JUSTICE. "Getting an Order of Protection". 2012. PDF File.

Pham, Jason. "15 Body-Positive Beyoncé Quotes to Remind You to Love Yourself." *StyleCaster*, StyleCaster, 18 Dec. 2018, stylecaster.com/beyonce-body-positive-quotes/.

"PUBLICATIONS." *NCJRS Abstract - National Criminal Justice Reference Service*, www.ncjrs.gov/App/Publications/abstract.aspx?ID=71030.

Representation2020.com. "Women's Underrepresentation in the Judiciary." *RepresentWomen*, www.representwomen.org/women_s_underrepresentation_in_the_judiciary.

Roufa, Timothy. "What to Know If You're Pursuing Criminal Justice Career." *The Balance Careers*, The Balance Careers, 1 Mar. 2020, www.thebalancecareers.com/what-is-criminal-justice-974588.

Rudall30. "Illustration of a superheroine in red cape with female symbol." iStock. Stock illustration ID:892841706 upload date:December 17, 2017

Seattle University College of Arts and Sciences, and Seattle University Center for the Study of Crime. "BADASSES: The Rise of Women in Criminal Justice." *Taylor & Francis*, www.tandfonline.com/doi/full/10.1080/08974454.2018.1468296?scroll=top&needAccess=true.

Sponsored; "NextStepU." *College Planning | Financial Aid and Advice to Plan for College*, NextStepU, www.nextstepu.com/reasons-choose-career-criminal-justice.art.

"The Public Servant." *Illinois State Bar Association,* www.isba.org/committees/governmentlawyers/newsletter/2013/06/becomingmoreawareafewtipsonkeepingy.

"Women's History Month." *United States Courts,* www.uscourts.gov/about-federal-courts/educational-resources/annual-observances/womens-history-month.

www.ingramcontent.com/pod-product-compliance
Lightning Source LLC
Chambersburg PA
CBHW051701090426
42736CB00013B/2484